DOMINOES

Nicholas Nickleby

LEVEL TWO 700 HEADWORDS

OXFORD
UNIVERSITY PRESS

Great Clarendon Street, Oxford OX2 6DP

Oxford University Press is a department of the University of Oxford.
It furthers the University's objective of excellence in research, scholarship, and education by publishing worldwide in

Oxford New York

Auckland Cape Town Dar es Salaam Hong Kong Karachi
Kuala Lumpur Madrid Melbourne Mexico City Nairobi
New Delhi Shanghai Taipei Toronto

With offices in

Argentina Austria Brazil Chile Czech Republic France Greece
Guatemala Hungary Italy Japan Poland Portugal Singapore
South Korea Switzerland Thailand Turkey Ukraine Vietnam

OXFORD and OXFORD ENGLISH are registered trade marks of Oxford University Press in the UK and in certain other countries

First published in Dominoes 2008

2023

25

ISBN: 978 0 19 424886 0 Book
ISBN: 978 0 19 463963 7 Book and Audio Pack

Printed in China

This book is printed on paper from certified and well-managed sources.

ACKNOWLEDGEMENTS

Cover photograph reproduced with permission from: Kobal Collection (Nicholas Nickleby 2002/ Hart-Sharp Ent./Simon Mein).

Illustrations by: Simon Gurr.

The publisher would like to thank the following for permission to reproduce photographs: Getty Images pp25 (The Strand early 20th Century/Popperfoto), 56 (Mr. And Mrs. Mantalini in Ralph Nickleby's Office. Illustration from the Charles Dickens novel Nicholas Nickleby by H.K. Browne known as Phiz/Universal History Archive), 57 (brawl between Sir Mulbery and his pupil. Illustration from the Charles Dickens novel Nicholas Nickleby by H.K. Browne known as Phiz/Universal History Archive); Kobal Collection pp47 (Nicholas Nickleby 2002/ Hart-Sharp Ent./Simon Mein), 59 (Nicholas Nickleby 2002/Hart-Sharp Ent./Simon Mein).

DOMINOES

Series Editors: Bill Bowler and Sue Parminter

Nicholas Nickleby

Charles Dickens

Text adaptation by Tim Herdon

Illustrated by Simon Gurr

Charles Dickens (1812–1870) was born in Portsmouth, England, and for most of his life lived in or near London. His family was poor, and he had to go out to work in a factory at the age of twelve. Dickens never forgot this difficult time, and many of his books describe the problems of poor people, especially poor children, and the wide differences between the rich and the poor. When he was older, Dickens started working for a newspaper and then wrote some of the most famous novels in English, including *Hard Times* which is also available as a Domino.

OXFORD
UNIVERSITY PRESS

ACTIVITIES

BEFORE READING

1 Here are some of the people in the story of Nicholas Nickleby's life and adventures. Match the sentences with the pictures.

Ralph Nickleby

Nicholas Nickleby

Kate Nickleby

Wackford Squeers

Smike

Newman Noggs

John Browdie

The Cheeryble brothers

a He's a nice young man who's looking for work, and he's Kate's brother.

b They're very rich and enjoy helping poor people.

c He was once rich but is now poor. He works for Ralph Nickleby.

d He's Nicholas's and Kate's rich uncle who lives in London.

e He's a poor young man, and he has a sad life.

f He's a big, strong but kind man who lives in the country.

g She's a nice young woman, and she's Nicholas's sister.

h He has a school but doesn't really teach his students anything.

2 Who helps Nicholas in the story, do you think? Who does he help? Who are his enemies?

Chapter one

A new start

When old Mr Nick Nickleby died at home in Devon in the south-west of England, he left many **debts** behind him. Once these were paid, his wife, his son – Nicholas – and his daughter – Kate – found themselves with little money and no house to live in. There was only one person that they could turn to for help: Ralph Nickleby, the children's **uncle**. Mrs Nickleby didn't really know him, but – because he was in the London **finance** business – he was rich and knew many people. Before her husband died, he said that Ralph would help them. So she wrote a letter to say that they were coming, and the very next day they all travelled to London.

Soon after they arrived, Ralph Nickleby came to the little house where they were staying. He wore fine clothes, but had cold eyes and a hard voice. He didn't look very **sad** about his brother's death.

debt money that you must pay back to someone

uncle your father's (or mother's) brother

finance to do with money

sad not happy

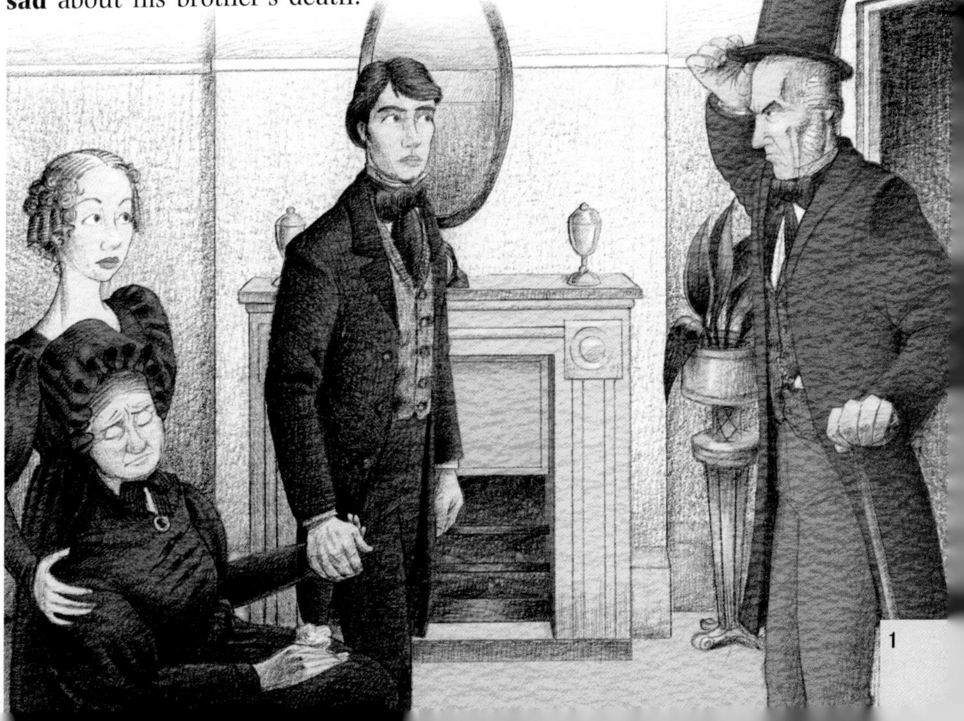

'How did he die?' he asked Mrs Nickleby.

'The doctors don't really know what the problem was. We think that perhaps he died of a broken **heart**,' replied Mrs Nickleby.

'I've heard of people dying of a broken neck, but a broken heart? Never. A man can't pay his debts and so he dies of a broken heart! Ha!' laughed Ralph Nickleby coldly.

'Some people have no heart to break,' said Nicholas to himself quietly.

'How old is this boy?' asked Ralph Nickleby, looking angrily at Nicholas.

'Nearly nineteen,' replied Mrs Nickleby.

'And how will you pay for your food now, boy?' Ralph Nickleby asked Nicholas.

'I shall not cost you or my mother anything at all,' replied Nicholas.

For a while Nicholas and his uncle looked at each other without speaking. The older man saw in front of him a young man who was kind and **honest**, and from that moment he **hated** him.

Then Ralph Nickleby talked with Mrs Nickleby about finding work for poor but beautiful Kate. Turning back to Nicholas, he showed him an **advertisement** in the newspaper that he had with him.

Mr Wackford Squeers – staying at the Snow Street **Inn** in North London – needs a teacher for his school in Yorkshire. Call today.

Yorkshire was far away, in the north-east of England, but Nicholas was excited.

'Perhaps our luck is changing!' he thought.

heart the centre of feeling in someone; this is in your chest and it sends the blood round your body

honest saying things that are true

hate not to love

advertisement you pay to put this information in a newspaper

inn an old name for a hotel near a road

'We must go and see Mr Squeers immediately, before he gives the job to another young man,' said Ralph Nickleby.

When Nicholas and his uncle arrived at the inn, Squeers was busy with some new students. He was a short man, about fifty years old. He had only one greeny-grey eye in his face, where people usually prefer two, and he looked very **strange** in his black suit, which was too long for him in the arms, and too short for him in the legs.

'Mr Squeers, this is my **nephew**, Mr Nicholas Nickleby. We're here because of your newspaper advertisement,' said Ralph Nickleby.

'He's too young to be a teacher,' Squeers said at once, looking at Nicholas.

But after talking quietly with Ralph Nickleby for a while, he turned back to Nicholas with a smile, saying, 'The job is yours. Our **coach** leaves at eight o'clock tomorrow morning. Be here early to help with the new students.'

'Certainly,' replied Nicholas. And to his uncle he said, 'I shall never forget how kind you've been.'

The next day, Nicholas said goodbye sadly to his sister and his mother at the inn.

'How will they **survive** without me?' he thought with a heavy heart.

Just before Nicholas got onto the coach, someone pushed a letter into his hand. It was Newman Noggs, Ralph Nickleby's **clerk**. Nicholas quickly put it into his pocket.

The journey to Yorkshire was long and hard, and they stopped at different inns on the way. Squeers ate a lot at every meal, but gave very little food to the students who were with him.

'He worries more about the cost of the meals than he does about those poor, hungry boys,' thought Nicholas.

strange not usual

nephew your sister's (or brother's) son

coach a kind of car with horses

survive to live through a difficult or dangerous time

clerk someone who does the writing work in an office

In the evening of the second day, they arrived in Yorkshire. There was snow everywhere, and in front of them was a long, low building with dark windows. It looked cold and unpleasant. This was the school – Dotheboys Hall.

Inside Mrs Squeers was waiting for them. She looked at Nicholas coldly, then turned to her husband.

'How is my Squeery?' she said.

'Very well my love,' replied Squeers. 'How are the cows and the other animals?'

'Very well.'

'And the boys?' asked Squeers.

'Oh, they're well, too,' replied Mrs Squeers quickly in a hard voice.

After that, they talked about parents who paid their debts to the school and parents who couldn't pay. Then Mrs Squeers put a cold supper on the table for her husband – and for Nicholas. Squeers ate and drank a lot; Nicholas had only a little. Then they all went to bed. Before he went to sleep on his bed on the floor upstairs, Nicholas took Noggs's letter from his pocket and read it:

My dear young man,

I know the world better than you. The place that you're going to isn't like any place that you know. If you ever need somewhere to stay in London, ask for me at the ***Crown*** *Inn, in Golden Square. They know me there. Don't think that I'm strange writing to you like this. I was once a* ***gentleman****, but I've come down in the world.*

Your friend,

Newman Noggs

crown a king or a queen wears this on their head

gentleman a man from a rich family who does not need to work

If Nicholas's first night at Dotheboys Hall was bad, the next day was worse. He soon saw that Mr and Mrs Squeers loved making the boys there **suffer**. Squeers **beat** them hard and often. He read their letters from home himself, telling them that their parents didn't love them and didn't want them back. The boys had no real lessons, but did jobs for Squeers in the school and its garden all day.

They were especially **cruel** to one boy – Smike. He was taller and older than the other boys at the school – perhaps eighteen or nineteen. His clothes were old and too small for him and he looked ill.

At the end of his first day, Nicholas found Smike working in the kitchen. He saw in the boy's eyes that he was afraid.

'Don't be afraid of me,' said Nicholas kindly.

'Oh, my poor heart will break, living here,' Smike cried.

'No it won't. There's always hope.'

'Not for me,' replied Smike. 'I've got no family or friends. It doesn't matter if I live or die. There's only **suffering** for me in this life.'

suffer to feel hurt or unhappy

beat (*past* **beat**, **beaten**) to hit strongly

cruel unkind and liking to hurt people

suffering when you feel hurt or unhappy

ACTIVITIES

READING CHECK

Are these sentences true or false? Tick the boxes.

		True	False
a	Mr Nick Nickleby dies of a broken neck.	☐	☑
b	Mr Squeers has a school in the north-east of England.	☐	☐
c	Mr Squeers gives Nicholas Nickleby a job as a teacher.	☐	☐
d	The journey to Yorkshire is short.	☐	☐
e	The school is warm and beautiful.	☐	☐
f	Mr and Mrs Squeers are cruel to the boys in their school.	☐	☐
g	Newman Noggs's letter says that Nicholas can't come to him for help.	☐	☐
h	Smike is very unhappy at Dotheboys Hall.	☐	☐

WORD WORK

1 Match the words in the coach with the pictures.

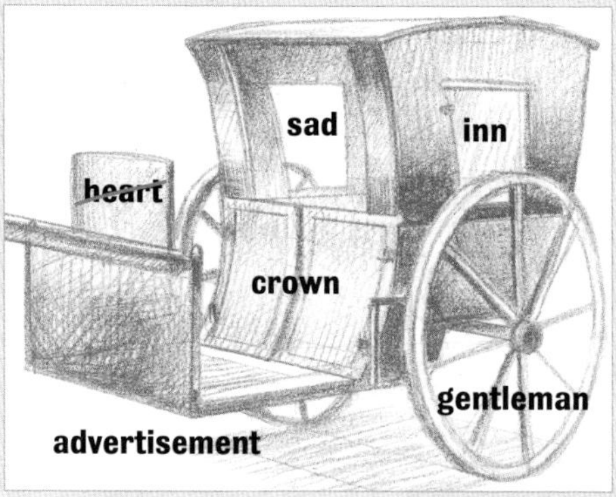

a

heart

f

______

b

______

c

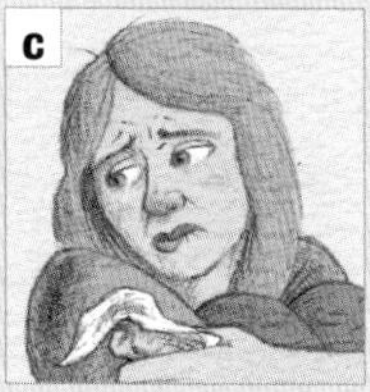

______

d

______

e

______

Complete the sentences with twelve other new words from Chapter 1 in the correct form.

a It's not good to have many debts.......... . You need to pay back money that you borrow quickly.

b It's difficult for a family to s.................. without money.

c My mother's brother, U.................. Jon, lives in Devon.

d Nicholas is h.................. : he always says what he thinks is true.

e Ralph Nickleby doesn't really love his family, and he h.................. Nicholas.

f Newman Noggs works as Ralph Nickleby's c.................. .

g People who are good with money enjoy working in the f.................. business.

h Mr and Mrs Squeers are more c.................. to Smike than to the other boys.

i Squeers likes b.................. the boys at the school with a big stick.

j Nicholas is Ralph Nickleby's n.................. .

k 'Dotheboys' isn't a very usual English name, and it's a s.................. name for a boy's school.

l Some people say that animals don't s.................., but when you hit an animal, you hurt it.

GUESS WHAT

What happens in the next chapter? Tick five boxes.

a We learn more about life at Dotheboys Hall. ☐

b We learn more about Ralph Nickleby's life in London. ☐

c Nicholas meets some new people in Yorkshire. ☐

d Life at Dotheboys Hall gets better. ☐

e Squeers beats Smike. ☐

f Nicholas beats Squeers. ☐

g Nicholas decides to stay at the school for a long time. ☐

h Nicholas decides to leave the school in the end. ☐

Chapter two

Life at Dotheboys Hall

After the night that they first met and talked in the kitchen, Smike followed Nicholas everywhere. But when Squeers saw this, he beat Smike more than before.

'They're harder with me than ever,' Smike cried one evening to Nicholas in the empty schoolroom.

'I know,' Nicholas replied, putting a hand on Smike's shoulder kindly. 'You'll be happier when I've gone.'

'Are you leaving?' asked Smike, suddenly worried.

'No,' said Nicholas. 'I was just thinking aloud.'

'But will you go one day?'

'Yes, one day I must go out into the world.'

'And can we meet – out in the world?' asked Smike.

'Of course,' said Nicholas. 'And I'll help you there and not make your life worse, as I've done here.'

Just then, Squeers arrived, and Smike disappeared.

Smike was not Nicholas's only worry at Dotheboys Hall. There was also Squeers's daughter, Fanny. One day – not long after Nicholas arrived – Fanny went into the schoolroom to get a pen. Nicholas gave her a friendly smile. 'What a wonderful smile he has,' she thought, and at once she decided that she was in love.

Soon after that, Fanny asked Nicholas to tea when Mrs Squeers was out. Fanny's best friend Tilda, and Tilda's **fiancé**, John Browdie, also came. There was bread and butter to eat, and Nicholas ate it very fast. When he saw this, John Browdie started laughing.

'You won't get fat if you stay in this school!' he said.

'John, don't speak to Mr Nickleby like that!' cried Fanny.

'Oh, Fanny. Shall we leave you and Mr Nickleby alone?' asked Tilda, laughing.

fiancé the man that a woman is going to marry

'Oh, no. Please don't go,' said Nicholas worriedly. He suddenly saw the way that things were going. Then, because he didn't want to **raise** Fanny's hopes of love, and because Browdie was a man of few words, he began to talk with Tilda. This made both Fanny and Browdie very angry.

In the end, Tilda and her fiancé went home, Fanny started crying, and Nicholas went off quickly up to bed. 'I must stop trying to be friendly to everyone!' he thought. 'It just gets me into trouble.'

One morning, not long after that, Squeers woke everyone by shouting from the kitchen downstairs, 'Are you going to sleep all day, you lazy dogs?'

'We're coming down now,' shouted Nicholas from the big long bedroom upstairs, where he and the boys all slept.

'Smike!' called Mrs Squeers. 'Come down here at once!' There was no reply.

Nicholas couldn't see Smike at all.

'He's not up here!' he cried.

'That's what you say!' shouted Squeers. 'I'm coming up to find him.'

'I think that he's run away,' said Nicholas when Squeers came upstairs.

raise to lift up

Squeers was very angry. 'How do you know that?' he asked. Now Mrs Squeers came upstairs, too.

'Smike has run away, my dear,' explained Squeers.

'That's no surprise to me!' said Mrs Squeers, looking at Nicholas with an **ugly** smile. 'You helped him!'

'I did not,' replied Nicholas hotly.

'I'll beat the life out of him when we catch him! Which way do you think he went?' Squeers asked his wife.

'Who knows? You take one coach and go **towards** York. I'll borrow another coach and go the other way,' replied Mrs Squeers.

For the rest of the day, Nicholas waited at the school with the other boys and worried.

In the evening, Squeers came back, but Smike wasn't with him.

'Someone will pay for this!' said Squeers angrily. 'I'm telling you, Nicholas.'

'It's nothing to do with me, **sir**,' said Nicholas, and he went to bed.

It was **clear** that Squeers wanted Smike back at the school just because the boy did lots of work there for nothing.

Early next morning, Nicholas heard a coach arriving at the front gate, and Mrs Squeers calling for her husband. Afraid of the worst, Nicholas looked through the window and saw Smike in the coach. His tired face was covered with **mud** and rain and he looked nearly dead. Mr Squeers came from the house and took him inside. He put him in the **cellar** and **locked** the door. He was **looking forward to** beating him later.

After lunch, Squeers told all the school to come to the classroom. When everyone was there, he brought Smike into the room, pulling him by his coat.

'Well, Smike, explain yourself!'

'Please, sir, **forgive** me!'

ugly not beautiful

towards nearer

sir you say this when you talk to a rich or important man

clear easy to understand

mud very wet ground

cellar a room under the ground at the bottom of a house

lock to close with a key

look forward to to think happily about something that is going to happen

forgive (*past* **forgave**, **forgiven**) to stop being angry with someone for something bad that they did

'Oh, yes, I'll forgive you – when I've finished beating the life out of you!'

'Ha! That's a good one,' shouted Mrs Squeers.

Squeers had a new **whip** to beat Smike with. He raised it, then brought it down hard on Smike's body. The poor boy screamed.

Then, suddenly, they heard a shout: 'Stop!'

'Who said that?' asked Squeers, looking round the room in great surprise.

'I did. This mustn't go on,' cried Nicholas, who was now very red in the face.

'Mustn't?' cried Squeers.

He took his hand from Smike's neck, raised his whip again, and used it to hit Nicholas in the face with all his **strength**. Nicholas at once pulled the whip from his hand, and began to beat him. Squeers screamed for help, but Nicholas went on beating him angrily. Mrs Squeers tried to pull her husband away, and Fanny hit Nicholas from behind with her hands, but they couldn't stop the attack. At last Nicholas left Squeers – not moving, but alive – to his wife and daughter. He couldn't see Smike anywhere, so he hurriedly put some clothes in a bag and left the house.

He decided to go at once to London. But how? It was far away and he had no money.

whip a special, long, thin stick that people use to hit animals

strength being strong

READING CHECK

Put these sentences in the correct order.

- **a** ☐ Nicholas can't find Smike and leaves for London.
- **b** ☐ Mrs Squeers brings Smike back to Dotheboys Hall.
- **c** ☐ Fanny asks Nicholas to tea with Tilda and John Browdie.
- **d** ☐ Nicholas beats Squeers.
- **e** ☐ Mr and Mrs Squeers go and look for Smike.
- **f** [1] Squeers starts beating Smike more than before.
- **g** ☐ Squeers beats Smike in front of all the boys.
- **h** ☐ Fanny decides that she is in love with Nicholas.
- **i** ☐ Smike runs away from Dotheboys Hall.

WORD WORK

1 Find new words from Chapter 2 in the whip.

2 What is Tilda's full name? Write the other letters in the whip in order to find it.

M _ _ _ _ _ _   _ _ _ _ _

3 Complete these sentences with the words from Activity 1.

- **a** He was very late but she ...forgave... him, and said that it didn't matter.
- **b** We ran down the hot beach .... the sea.
- **c** She was tired, and didn't have the .... to carry her bags upstairs.
- **d** Her .... is French. They're planning to marry next year.
- **e** Please .... your hand if you know the answer.
- **f** He's a very .... man with a big nose, ears and mouth, and small eyes.
- **g** I'm .... to the party on Monday. It's going to be great.

Correct the boxed words in these sentences.

a He hit his horse with a ~~ship.~~ whip

b After he walked across the wet field there was mad on his shoes.

c We've got a big empty caller under our house.

d I can't understand what she's saying. It's not clean to me what she wants.

e He closed the door and licked it.

f 'Have you lost your way, sit?' the policeman asked him.

GUESS WHAT

What happens in the next chapter? Tick the boxes.

	Yes	Perhaps	No
a Squeers comes and takes Nicholas back to the school.	☐	☐	☐
b Squeers becomes very ill and dies in Yorkshire.	☐	☐	☐
c Nicholas walks all the way to London.	☐	☐	☐
d Smike travels to London with Nicholas.	☐	☐	☐
e Ralph Nickleby is happy to see Nicholas again.	☐	☐	☐

Mr Squeers

Smike

Nicholas

Ralph Nickleby

Chapter three

The road to London

After walking away from Dotheboys Hall for some time, Nicholas saw John Browdie on the road in front of him, carrying a big stick.

'Oh no! Will he hit me with his stick?' thought Nicholas. 'After what happened at tea the other day.'

'Good evening, young gentleman,' said John Browdie when they met.

'Look, I'm sorry about what happened when you came to tea,' said Nicholas. 'I didn't mean anything by it. Will you forget it, and shake hands?'

'Of course,' said Browdie, and he gave Nicholas his hand. 'But what's happened to your face?'

Nicholas told him everything. When John Browdie heard about Nicholas beating Squeers, he suddenly gave a great shout of **joy**.

'That's the best news that I've heard in twenty years,' he laughed. 'But what will you do now?'

'I'm going to walk to London.'

'Good luck. It's a long way to walk. Here, take some money, and my stick. You'll need it,' said Browdie kindly, and he gave Nicholas a pound and his stick, and then went on his way. Stick in hand, Nicholas walked off towards London.

He slept that night in the cheapest inn that he could find. He walked all the next day, but at night he could find only a **barn** to sleep in. After a deep sleep, he woke up early the next morning, and saw Smike standing in front of him.

'Smike! How did you come here?'

'When you left the school, I followed you all yesterday. I slept in this barn last night, too. I didn't want you to see me, but this morning you woke up too quickly for me to hide.

joy a very happy feeling

barn a big building on a farm where you keep food for the animals

Please take me to London with you. I'll do anything. I'll be your servant. I just want to be with you.'

'Of course you can come with me, but not as my **servant**. We'll go out into the world together, and what we find there will be for both of us.'

So they started their long walk together. On the way, Nicholas thought, 'We'll go and look for Newman Noggs at the Crown Inn. He'll tell me where I can find Kate and my mother.'

Some days later, late at night, Newman Noggs was at home when he heard visitors at his door. Opening it, he saw Nicholas and Smike standing there, both **exhausted**. He asked them in, and gave them something to eat and drink. Soon after that, they both fell asleep.

The next morning Nicholas told Noggs their story.

'I knew most of that already,' said Noggs, when he finished. 'Fanny Squeers wrote a long letter about it all to your uncle, you see.'

'And does it tell the same story?'

servant a person who works for someone rich

exhausted very tired

'Not really. The letter says that you used bad language, that you nearly killed Squeers, that you attacked her mother and herself, and that you stole one of Mrs Squeers's rings.'

'But that's not true!' shouted Nicholas. 'No one who knows me could believe it. I'll go and see my uncle and explain what really happened.'

'Wait a minute,' replied Newman, 'Ralph Nickleby hates you, so he'll say that he believes what's in the letter. You must go and see your mother and sister and explain things to them before your uncle talks to them. I'll show you the way to their house.'

But when they arrived at his mother's house, Ralph Nickleby was already there. Kate ran to Nicholas, and **embraced** him.

'Oh Nicholas, you're back!' she cried, full of joy at seeing her brother again.

embrace to take lovingly in your arms

'Your uncle has told us terrible things about you and Mr Squeers,' said Mrs Nickleby sadly. 'Are they true?'

'No, mother, it didn't happen the way that my uncle told you,' replied Nicholas.

'So you didn't beat Mr Squeers with a whip? And you didn't take a boy away from the school?' said Ralph Nickleby, with a small, cold smile.

'Yes, I **admit** that I did these things, but I did them to stop the suffering of a poor, **innocent** boy,' replied Nicholas.

'When you came from Devon, I **looked after** all of you,' said Ralph Nickleby, turning to Nicholas's mother. 'Now see how your son pays me back for my **kindness**!' And with these words, he left the house before Nicholas could hit him angrily in the face.

'How can he talk like that?' cried Kate after he left.

'What do you mean?' asked Nicholas.

'While you were in Yorkshire, a friend of his, Sir Mulberry Hawk, **treated** me very badly. I met him at a dinner that our uncle invited me to, although I didn't want to go. After dinner, I had to go and lie down because I wasn't feeling very well. Sir Mulberry came into the room where I lay, and tried to **kiss** me. I told him to stop, but he didn't. In the end, I had to run out of the room to escape from him.'

'If I ever see this Mulberry Hawk, I'll teach him a lesson!' said Nicholas angrily.

'Later I told our uncle everything,' went on Kate. 'I said that Sir Mulberry needed to say sorry. But Uncle Ralph explained that he couldn't possibly ask him to do that because he was an important business friend.'

'So this is how our uncle looks after us!' said Nicholas to himself. 'He **lets** his friends do anything that they like with his niece, because it's good for business. And he sends me to be a teacher at the worst school in England. What a "kind" and "helpful" man our uncle is!'

admit to say openly that you did something

innocent having done nothing wrong

look after to do things for someone or something that needs help

kindness kind feelings; something kind that someone does

treat to speak and act towards

kiss to touch lovingly with your mouth

let to agree to someone doing something, and not try to stop them

READING CHECK

What do they say?

a Take some money and my stick.

b I just want to be with you.

c ~~Will you forget it, and shake hands?~~

d Now see how your son pays me back for my kindness.

e Sir Mulberry tried to kiss me.

f What a 'kind' and 'helpful' man our uncle is.

g Her letter says that you nearly killed Squeers.

h I don't know what to think!

1 [c] Nicholas says to John Browdie.
2 [ ] John Browdie says to Nicholas.
3 [ ] Smike says to Nicholas.
4 [ ] Newman Noggs tells Nicholas.
5 [ ] Mrs Nickleby says to Nicholas.
6 [ ] Ralph Nickleby says to Mrs Nickleby.
7 [ ] Kate tells Nicholas.
8 [ ] Nicholas says to himself after he hears his sister's story.

WORD WORK

Use the words in the pen to complete Nicholas's diary.

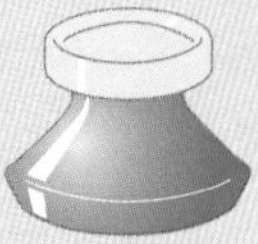

admit barns embrace exhausted innocent joy kindness kiss lets looked after ~~servant~~ treated

Sunday

Smike came with me on the journey to London. He wanted to be my a) ..servant....., but I said that we would travel together as friends. It was cold on the way, and because we had no money, we often slept in b) .... We walked for days with little food, and when we arrived, we felt c) .... But what a d) .... it was to see Kate and Mother, and to e) .... them lovingly again! My uncle was there, too. He wasn't happy to see me, and told me about Fanny's letter. None of it's true, of course, but she'll never f) .... that. My uncle hasn't g) .... Kate well while I was away. His friend Sir Mulberry Hawk h) .... her very badly. He tried to i) ....her. And Kate is so young and j) ....! I feel angry just thinking about it. I thought that there was more k) .... in my uncle's heart than that. And Mother is afraid of him, and l) .... him do what he wants. I must get Kate and Mother away from him. And I must find some work.

GUESS WHAT

What happens in the next chapter? Match the sentences with the people.

a Nicholas
b A strange man
c Nicholas, Kate, Mrs Nickleby and Smike
d Smike
e Squeers

1 helps Nicholas.
2 feels happy in London.
3 wants to take Smike to Yorkshire with him.
4 move into a new house in London.
5 looks for a job in London.

Chapter four

New friends and old friends

The morning after he arrived in London, Nicholas went to the **Employment Office** to look for a job. There were many advertisements in the window of the office for lots of different jobs: servants, clerks, teachers and more. While Nicholas was looking at these advertisements, he saw a short, fat older man with kind, smiling eyes looking at them too, and they started talking.

The man was very surprised that Nicholas, a young man from a good family, and a good student, didn't have a job. Nicholas told him a little about himself, about the death of his father, and about his worries for his mother and sister. The little man listened to him carefully and quietly, sometimes asking him a question or two. But when Nicholas told him about his uncle Ralph, and the way that he treated Kate, the man stood up very quickly and told him, 'Come with me!'

Without another word, they took a coach to the business part of the **city** and went into a large building. Over the door there was a **sign** that said, 'Cheeryble Brothers'.

'What's the meaning of this journey? And what does this little man want with me? It's a mystery,' thought Nicholas. 'But perhaps something good will come out of it.'

Inside the building, the man asked Nicholas to wait a little. He went into an office, and Nicholas could hear two men talking seriously about something for a moment or two. The strange thing was that their voices were **exactly** the same. After a short time, the door opened, and the man from the Employment Office asked Nicholas to go in.

'Young man, this is my **twin** brother Ned Cheeryble, and I'm Charles Cheeryble,' he said.

Nicholas's mouth fell open. Charles Cheeryble wasn't

Employment Office a place where you look for a job

city (*plural* **cities**) a big and important town

sign writing in a place that tells people about something important

exactly in all ways

twin one of a pair of brothers or sisters who are born on the same day exactly as short or as fat as his brother, Ned, but in every other way they were the same. They had the same smiling eyes, the same clothes, even the same white hats. Charles's hat was now in his hand, and Ned's was up on the **coat rack** on the wall. It was clear that they were twins.

'Young man, when we first came to this great city, we had no money in our coat pockets and no shoes on our feet,' said Ned.

'Since then we've started this business, and now we've become very rich,' said Charles.

'These days we enjoy helping other people with our money,' Ned went on.

'And we'd like to help you. We need a clever young man to help with the **accounts** for our business,' said Charles. 'Our old accounts clerk isn't getting any younger, you see.'

'And we think that you're just the right person for the job,' finished Ned.

Nicholas's mouth fell open again.

'I can't thank you enough for your kindness. I don't know what to say,' he began.

'Then don't say anything,' said Charles.

coat rack something on the wall on which people can put coats when they take them off

accounts writing in a book that shows how money goes out of and comes into a business

'Now, come on. It's all agreed,' said Ned. 'You'll start tomorrow at eight o'clock in the morning, and I'll show you then what you need to do.'

The Cheeryble brothers went on talking together after Nicholas left.

'Charles, is anyone living in that little house that we have in Bow?'

'No, Ned, it's empty.'

'Then perhaps Nicholas could live in it with his family. And they could pay a smaller **rent** than usual, couldn't they, Charles?'

'Or no rent, Ned. We're so rich, and they need the money more than us, after all.'

'You're so right, Charles. Let's tell Nicholas the good news tomorrow morning.'

Nicholas started work for the Cheerybles the next day. The twins helped Nicholas a lot, and he quickly learned how to do the accounts. The brothers liked having a laugh with each other, and with those around them, and Nicholas enjoyed his work.

The next two weeks were a very happy time. Two days after Nicholas started work, Nicholas, Kate, Mrs Nickleby, and Smike moved into the little house in Bow. The Cheerybles were again very helpful: they sent men to help with the moving, and they also gave the Nicklebys some pieces of **furniture** for their new home.

Every day, when Nicholas came back from work, he found some new change in the house. Kate worked quietly all day to make their little home comfortable. Mrs Nickleby talked a lot about all the work to do in the house, but did very little of it herself.

Smike worked in the garden, and made it look very beautiful. The poor boy was happy for the first time in his

rent to give money every month for somewhere to live

furniture tables and chairs, for example

life; at last he had a family. He began to eat more, and to look less thin. And you could see the change in his face, too; he wasn't afraid or lonely any more.

grab to take someone or something quickly in your hands

But after two happy weeks, something happened that changed everything. Smike was walking home from the park one afternoon when suddenly someone **grabbed** his shoulder. He turned round. Before he knew exactly what was happening, that same someone pushed him into a coach. It was Squeers.

'What a piece of luck to find you here,' Squeers said, smiling cruelly.

'I must go home!' cried Smike, afraid.

'Oh, yes, I'll take you home – to Dotheboy's Hall in Yorkshire! Mrs Squeers will be very surprised to see you. Now I've never beaten a boy in a coach before, but I must say that I'm looking forward to it.'

Then Squeers hit Smike again and again with all his strength. The poor boy fell to the floor with his head in his hands and, just then, the coach began to move away fast.

ACTIVITIES

READING CHECK

Match the first and second parts of these sentences.

a Nicholas Nickleby goes
b Charles Cheeryble takes
c The Cheeryble brothers give
d Ned and Charles also let
e Mrs Nickleby doesn't help
f Kate Nickleby works hard
g Smike is happy
h Squeers says that he's taking

1 very much in the house.
2 Smike back to Dotheboys Hall.
3 Nicholas to his office in a coach.
4 for the first time in his life.
5 the Nicklebys live in their house.
6 to look for work.
7 to make the house beautiful.
8 Nicholas a job.

WORD WORK

1 These words don't match the pictures. Correct them.

a ~~sign~~ coat rack ....

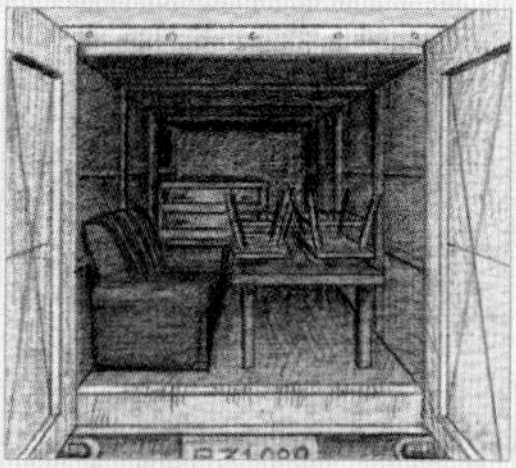

b twins ....

c coat rack ....

d Employment Office ....

e furniture ....

ACTIVITIES

Complete these sentences with words from Chapter 4 in the correct form.

a Nicholas is exactly the kind of young man that the Cheerybles are looking for.

b They need Nicholas to do the _ _ _ _ _ _ _ _ _ for their business.

c They don't want him to pay any _ _ _ _ for the house in Bow.

d Squeers _ _ _ _ _ _ Smike in the street.

e London in the 1840s was a very dirty _ _ _ _.

GUESS WHAT

What happens in the next chapter? Tick four boxes.

a Smike jumps out of the coach. ☐

b Squeers takes Smike to his inn in London. ☐

c Smike tells Squeers where Nicholas is living. ☐

d Squeers beats Smike to death. ☐

e John Browdie helps Smike to run away. ☐

f John Browdie helps Squeers to take Smike back to Yorkshire. ☐

g Smike runs away from Squeers but loses his way. ☐

h Smike walks all night before he arrives at the house in Bow. ☐

Chapter five

Another long walk

The coach with Squeers and Smike in it arrived after a while at the inn where Squeers was staying. He pushed Smike inside, and got the key of the room next to his, which was empty. Then he pulled Smike upstairs, pushed the poor boy into the empty room, and locked the door behind him. His **plan** was to leave Smike there until next morning, and then take him back to Yorkshire.

A short time later, another coach arrived at the inn. In it were Fanny Squeers, her friend Tilda, and John Browdie, now Tilda's husband. All three were in London to see the great city for the first time, and they were staying at the same inn as Squeers, who met them downstairs.

'You'll never **believe** who's here. He's an old friend,' he said, smiling strangely.

'Nicholas Nickleby?' asked Fanny.

'No, but nearly.'

'Smike then!'

'Yes, it's young Smike, the boy who forgot to say goodbye when he left.'

'Where is he?' asked John Browdie with some interest.

'I've got him locked away in the empty room next to my room upstairs,' smiled Squeers.

Just then, dinner arrived. While they were eating, they talked about Smike and Nicholas. Squeers drank a lot of wine. Slowly the conversation moved to other things. Tilda and Fanny began talking about the shops in London that they wanted to see.

Suddenly John Browdie started **coughing**. His face went red and he couldn't stop.

'What is it, John?' said Tilda. 'Shall I call a doctor?'

plan to want to do something; to get something ready before doing it

believe to think something is true

cough to make a noise in your throat

'No, I'm fine,' he answered, but he went on coughing, and his face got redder and redder.

'Do you need to lie down for a few minutes?' she asked.

'Yes, go and lie down. Don't call a doctor; they're very expensive in London,' said Squeers.

And so Tilda helped John Browdie to walk upstairs. After a few minutes, she came down again, saying that he was asleep in bed.

'Good,' said Squeers. 'Sleep's cheaper than a doctor.' And he **poured** himself some more wine.

Now alone upstairs, John Browdie went to the room where Smike was. The key was in the lock on the outside of the door. He turned the key quietly, and opened the door. Quickly he put his hand over Smike's mouth to stop him from speaking.

'Don't be afraid,' he told Smike. 'I'm going to help you to run away.'

Taking a **screwdriver** out of his pocket, he took the lock out of the door, and then put both the lock and the screwdriver on the floor. Then, turning to Smike, he said:

pour to put liquid – like water or wine – from a bottle into a glass

screwdriver you can put screws into or take them out of something by turning this one way or the other way

'You did that before you ran away. Is that clear?'

Smike didn't understand.

'Look, I don't want Squeers to know that I helped you to run away. My wife is a friend of his daughter's. Now do you see?'

'Yes, now I do,' replied Smike.

'Good. So come with me.'

Walking as quietly as they could, they went downstairs. Squeers, Tilda and Fanny were still eating their dinner. They were all laughing at a story that Tilda was telling. John Browdie opened the front door quietly. Smike, looking at him thankfully, ran out into the night. John Browdie, laughing to himself, went upstairs and lay down on his bed again.

Now free from Squeers, Smike ran as fast as he could. He was so afraid that for the first hour he ran towards the west, the wrong way. He understood his mistake when he saw that he was going out of London. So then he turned and walked towards the east. He needed to ask the way often, but he never stopped walking.

The first light of the morning sun was in the sky when he arrived at Bow. He was home at last! As soon as Nicholas heard Smike's knock, he opened the front door. And when he saw that Smike was outside – cold, dirty, and exhausted – he embraced him.

Kate and Mrs Nickleby also came down to find out who was calling so early, and it was a very fine thing to see the joy on everybody's faces now that Smike was back with them once again.

All three of them were worried when they heard that Squeers was back in town, and that he wanted to take Smike back to Yorkshire with him, but they were all very happy to hear of the poor boy's escape from the inn with John Browdie's help.

Not long after Smike's adventure with Squeers, a strange thing happened at the Cheeryble Brothers' offices. Nicholas needed to show a letter to Charles. Knocking at his office door, he heard no reply.

'I'll leave it on his desk for him to look at when he comes back,' thought Nicholas, opening the door.

He was surprised to see that Charles was in his office. He was talking to a young woman who was sitting in front of him. She was eighteen or nineteen, and very beautiful. She was also crying a lot, and then suddenly, she **fainted**.

Charles asked Nicholas to leave the office immediately, and to send in his brother, Ned. Nicholas was so surprised by the **sight** of this beautiful girl that he could only stand looking at her without moving or speaking. Just then, Ned hurried into the office.

'My dear Nicholas,' he said. 'You must leave the room at once. Don't worry about this young **lady**. She'll be well again soon. Leave us, I **beg** you.'

'But who is she?' Nicholas asked himself while he was leaving the room.

faint to fall down suddenly because you are weak, ill, afraid or horrified

sight something that you see

lady a woman from a good family

beg to ask for something very strongly

READING CHECK

Are these sentences true or false? Tick the boxes.

		True	False
a	Squeers keeps Smike in a room with the door open.	☐	☑
b	Squeers, Fanny, Tilda, and John Browdie have supper downstairs.	☐	☐
c	The others think that Browdie is ill when he doesn't stop laughing.	☐	☐
d	Tilda helps Browdie to sit down in his room.	☐	☐
e	Using a screwdriver, Browdie takes the lock out of the door to Smike's room.	☐	☐
f	Outside the inn Smike immediately runs towards London.	☐	☐
g	Nicholas, Kate, and Mrs Nickleby are very happy when they see Smike again.	☐	☐
h	At work, Nicholas sees a rich young woman.	☐	☐

WORD WORK

Find the words in the screws to complete the sentences.

a I can't ..believe.. that you're phoning me. I haven't heard from you for ages.

b Our .... is to visit New York next summer.

c First .... the milk into the cup and then the tea.

d Arthur always .... when he sees blood.

e My favourite .... in Istanbul is the Ayasofya.

f When Julie's grandad .... her to sing for him, she always says 'no'.

g Who's the young .... in the gold dress, James?

ACTIVITIES

GUESS WHAT

Who does what in the next chapter? Match the sentences with the people.

a . . . keeps quiet about the young lady.

b . . . tells Nicholas how he helped Smike run away.

c . . . says that he wants to stay with Nicholas.

d . . . tries to find out more about the young lady.

e . . . takes a man who says that he's Smike's father to see Smike.

f . . . tries to grab Smike again.

1 *Nicholas* ☐

2 *Ned Cheeryble* ☐

3 *John Browdie* ☐

4 *Ralph Nickleby* ☐

5 *Squeers* ☐

6 *Smike* ☐

Chapter six

Nicholas in love

For an hour after leaving Charles's office, Nicholas could do no work. He sat at his desk, thinking about the beautiful young woman still inside with Charles and Ned. The time passed very slowly. Then at last, Ned Cheeryble came out of Charles's office.

'Is she better?' asked Nicholas.

'Who?' replied Ned.

'The young lady.'

'Oh, yes, she's fine now.'

Nicholas tried to find out more about her from him, but Ned was strangely silent all that afternoon.

During the next few days, the young lady came and went many times. Her talks with the Cheeryble brothers were always secret, and they always happened inside Ned's or Charles's office, behind closed doors. Nicholas often tried to find out more about her, but the Cheeryble brothers never talked about her with him. Day after day Nicholas thought of her more and more. He wanted to tell his sister about her. But what could he say? He didn't even know the young woman's name.

But in the middle of all this, Nicholas didn't forget his friends. The Browdies were leaving London soon to go back to Yorkshire. So he invited them to dinner. They came to the house the next night, and at first it was a happy evening. They talked for a long time about Squeers and Smike, and how Browdie helped Smike to escape. They all laughed when Browdie described how angry Squeers looked when he found the lock, the screwdriver, the empty bed and no Smike in the room. Smike laughed more than the rest. Mrs Nickleby

thanked John Browdie more than twenty times for treating her son so kindly in Yorkshire.

It was eleven o'clock, and the Browdies were leaving, when they heard a loud knock at the door.

'Who could that be so late?' said Mrs Nickleby, going to open it. Outside the door stood Ralph Nickleby, with Squeers, and a third man. They all came at once into the house.

'I've got something important to say to you all,' said Ralph Nickleby.

'You have *nothing* to say to us, and we have *nothing* to say to you,' said Nicholas angrily, walking towards his uncle. John Browdie stopped him.

'Let's hear what he has to say,' he said.

'Yes, listen. You'll find it very interesting,' said Squeers.

'It's very simple,' said Ralph Nickleby. 'My nephew Nicholas took Smike away from school in Yorkshire.' Ralph Nickleby now pointed at the third man. 'This gentleman here is Mr Snawley. He's young Smike's father, and he wants Smike to go back to that school.'

Mr Snawley then walked over to Smike. 'My dearest son, come to your father,' he said while he embraced him. Nicholas and John Browdie looked at each other in surprise.

'If anyone doesn't believe what I've just said, here are some papers which show that it's all true,' said Ralph Nickleby, pulling some papers out of his coat pocket. Nicholas looked at them quickly.

'If these papers are real,' he said. 'Mr Snawley and Smike's mother **separated** when Smike was only a year old. He's not seen his son since then – until today.'

Suddenly Smike spoke, 'I don't want to go with that man. I don't know him. I want to stay here with you, Nicholas.'

'But I want my son,' said Snawley.

'Your son, if he really is that,' said Nicholas, '**chooses** for himself. And he chooses to stay, so he'll stay.'

'Listen to how he speaks!' said Squeers, moving forward to grab Smike. Seeing this, John Browdie stood in front of Smike. He pushed Squeers back hard with one of his big hands, and Squeers fell back at once onto Ralph Nickleby, who was just behind him. Then Ralph Nickleby fell over, too.

When they got up from the floor, Nicholas said, 'Now leave this house at once and don't come back.'

'You'll be sorry for what you've done tonight. You can't come between a man and his son,' Ralph Nickleby said, raising his voice.

separate to stop being together

choose (*past* **chose**, **chosen**) to decide which one of a number of things you want

Then the three men left, shouting many other angry **threats** behind them while they were going out of the front door.

That night Nicholas slept very little. Could Snawley and Squeers really decide on poor Smike's future? The next day he told Charles Cheeryble about Snawley, and about his uncle's threats.

'Don't be afraid of these men,' said Charles. 'Early this morning your uncle came to see me, too. He tried to make me think badly of you, but I didn't listen to him. I'll do everything I can to help you, your family, and Smike – so don't worry. Smike will stay with you.'

'Your words have given me strength. How can I ever thank you enough for all that you've done?' asked Nicholas.

'By not talking about it, my dear friend,' replied Charles. 'Now, I'm going to give you a special and secret job.' Charles was nervous, and he began to walk up and down the room while he spoke.

'Please tell me what it is,' said Nicholas. 'I'll try my very best to do it well.'

'Do you remember that very sad young lady who was in my office a few days ago?'

threat a bad thing that you say you will do to someone to make them feel afraid

'Yes, of course I do,' replied Nicholas.

'Her name's Madeline. Many, many years ago I loved her mother. But, sadly, in the end she married another man, whose name is Bray. Their life together was not happy, because he had many debts. Near the end of her life, she came to me asking for my help with some of these debts, and I was truly happy to help her. Bray's been very ill for many years now, and can't do very much to help himself.'

'And how does he treat his daughter?' asked Nicholas.

'Very badly. He thinks only of himself, never of her. Now, when the mother died, she asked her only daughter – Madeline – to look after her father. Madeline has never forgotten this. But there are still many of her father's debts to pay, and Madeline finds it very hard. This is where my brother Ned and I are trying to help. Madeline is an **artist**, and we buy her pictures, usually for much more than the real **price**. This is the only money that she has. But we don't want Bray to know who is buying the pictures, because he hates me, and has always hated me. Your job is to go to Bray's house with the money, and to come back with the pictures. You mustn't tell Bray that you've come from the Cheerybles, of course.'

'I understand,' said Nicholas. He went back to his work with two words sounding in his head: 'Madeline Bray!' Those two words were like music to Nicholas's ears.

The next day Nicholas went to the Brays' house and bought one of Madeline's pictures. While he was there, Bray shouted at him.

'Don't think that we need your help,' he cried. 'We come from a better family than you, my daughter and I.'

At the door Madeline said, 'Please don't think badly of my father. He's ill and suffers so much. And please don't say anything of this to the Cheeryble brothers. They're so kind to us.'

artist a person who makes pictures

price the money that you must pay to buy something

'Ask me to do anything that you like. I'm your servant,' answered Nicholas.

At once Madeline turned her head, began to cry, and hurried back into the house.

One afternoon, not long after Nicholas started visiting the Brays' house, Newman Noggs came to see him at home.

'It's very good to see you, my friend,' said Nicholas, showing Noggs into the front room.

'And you, Nicholas. But I bring bad news, I'm afraid. I believe that you know Madeline Bray?'

'Yes, I do. Why? Has something happened to her?' asked Nicholas worriedly.

'Not yet. But she's in great danger. This morning I **overheard** a conversation between your uncle and Mr Arthur Gride.'

'Who's he?' asked Nicholas.

'He's a **moneylender**, like your uncle. He's an ugly old man, with no friends and no kindness in his heart. Madeline's father borrowed a lot of money from him in the past, and one day he must pay it all back. Gride has never been married and now that he's an old man, he wants only one thing.'

Suddenly Nicholas's heart went cold.

'Gride has agreed to **cancel** Bray's debt if Bray gives him Madeline's hand in **marriage**,' Noggs went on.

'No! That can't be true!' cried Nicholas.

overhear (*past* **overheard**) to hear a conversation without the people talking knowing that you are there

moneylender a person that people go to when they want to borrow money

cancel to stop something that was planned

marriage when two people are married

READING CHECK

Correct eight more mistakes in the chapter summary.

Nicholas tries to find out more about the young gentleman, but the Cheerybles are strangely quiet about him. One evening the Browdies come to breakfast. When they are leaving, Ralph Nickleby and Squeers come to the house with a third man called Mr Snawley. Ralph Nickleby says that Snawley is Smike's uncle and that he wants Smike to go back to Devon. But Nicholas and John Browdie stop them from taking Smike away. When he hears about this the next day, Charles Cheeryble tells Nicholas that he will do nothing to help him. He also asks Nicholas for help: he has to buy stories from Madeline Bray, the beautiful young lady, to help pay her mother's debts. When Nicholas sees Madeline at her house, he tells her that he will do anything for her. But later Newman Noggs tells him that Madeline is going to separate from an old man called Mr Arthur Gride.

WORD WORK

1 Find seven more words from Chapter 6 in the wordsquare.

S	M	I	R	T	C	O	E	C
C	O	S	A	I	L	G	I	H
A	M	E	M	N	A	U	R	O
N	U	P	F	I	I	S	N	O
C	Q	A	R	T	I	S	T	S
E	T	R	W	I	E	H	W	E
L	A	A	D	A	C	M	H	F
M	O	T	T	H	R	E	A	T
O	V	E	R	H	E	A	R	F

ACTIVITIES

Use the words from Activity 1 in the correct form to complete the sentences.

a What kind of chocolate would you like? Go on! Take the box and ..choose.......... .

b When Mum and Dad .... , and Dad left home, I stayed with Mum.

c Don't use .... like 'I'll kill you!' or 'You'll be sorry!' with young children.

d Frida Kahlo was a Mexican ....; her pictures are strange but great.

e What's the .... of that picture over there? Is it expensive?

f Last night I .... two women talking behind me on the bus. It was very interesting!

g Today's plane to Cairo has been .... But you can fly tomorrow.

h My parent's .... is a good one, They're happy together.

GUESS WHAT

What happens in the next chapter? Complete each sentence with a name.

Mr Gride *Mr Bray* *Smike* *Madeline* *Ralph Nickleby* *Nicholas*

a .... dies in his daughter's arms.

b .... is stopped from marrying Madeline.

c .... becomes ill and has Kate as a nurse.

d .... becomes ill and has to go to Devon.

e .... helps Madeline and Smike.

f .... loses lots of money.

Chapter seven

Night comes on

'I'm afraid that it *is* true, Nicholas,' went on Noggs. 'Your uncle has agreed to talk to Bray about Madeline for Gride. If Bray agrees to the marriage with his daughter, Gride will pay your uncle a small part of the cancelled debt. This means that —'

'Gride is planning to buy a young wife, and that my uncle is helping him, for money!' said Nicholas. 'But will Bray agree?'

'I know Bray. He's a man with no heart. He won't think of his daughter's **happiness**. He's old and he just wants to **get rid of** his debts before he dies.'

'I won't let this happen. I must stop it,' said Nicholas.

The next morning Ralph Nickleby was at Gride's house.

'Yesterday evening I spoke to Bray.'

'And?'

'He's agreed to the marriage in two days' time.'

'And what about Madeline?' asked Gride.

happiness a happy feeling

get rid of (*past* **got rid of**) to become free of something, to throw something away

'Don't worry about her. She'll agree to it if her father says yes,' answered Ralph Nickleby. 'Come to my place at seven the day after tomorrow, and don't visit her between now and then. You've seen too much of her lately. That's dangerous. She doesn't love you, and we don't want anything to change our plans.'

That afternoon Nicholas again went to the Brays' house. He took a small picture from Madeline, and gave her five pounds for it. Her hand was shaking when she took the money from him.

At the door he spoke to her quietly, 'Madeline, I know about the marriage with Gride. And I beg you not to do it.'

'How do you know about it?' she asked, her face white.

'It doesn't matter. But please don't marry Gride just because your father tells you to. Your happiness is important, too.'

'But I must do what my father tells me. There are more important things than my happiness. I beg you not to speak of this any more.'

Just then, they heard Bray's voice from his room upstairs. 'If you've given Madeline the money, young man, why are you still here? And you needn't come back again. Madeline won't need to sell any more pictures soon. Goodbye.'

Madeline ran back into the house, closing the door.

'This won't be easy,' thought Nicholas.

Two days later Ralph Nickleby and Gride went to the Brays' house for the **wedding**. A servant opened the door to them, and they waited downstairs. After a short time Bray came into the room. He asked to speak to Ralph Nickleby alone.

'Madeline was very ill last night. Do you think that I'm cruel to marry my daughter to Gride? He's so old after all.'

'No, no, I think it's a fine plan,' answered Ralph Nickleby quickly.

wedding the day when two people marry

'I thought that it was when we spoke before. But now I'm not so sure.'

'Don't worry. Gride won't live for many more years. And when he dies, she'll be rich, and then she can marry any man that she chooses.'

'Yes, that's a good way to think of it. Well, I must go and see her.' And he went upstairs again.

Suddenly there was a knock at the front door, and a moment later Nicholas and Kate hurried into the room.

'What are *you* doing here?' asked Ralph Nickleby.

'We've come to stop your plan,' said Nicholas.

Nicholas and his uncle looked long and hard at each other like two old enemies.

'Why did you come here with your sister?' Ralph Nickleby asked Nicholas. 'It'll make me very happy to push you out into the street, but I don't want to hurt your sister. So Kate, please leave at once.'

'It's strange that today you're worried about hurting me,' replied Kate. 'You weren't worried about me when I told you about Sir Mulberry Hawk. You said that business came first. And now you and Gride are using poor Madeline to pay a debt. Admit it – it's just business to you, isn't it?'

'You're making a great mistake, my dear young niece. Madeline is going to be married to Mr Gride today. That's all. And if you don't leave now, you and your brother will get hurt,' said Ralph Nickleby coldly.

'I won't leave this house until we take Madeline out of it,' replied Kate.

Suddenly they heard a **thump** and a scream of, 'He's dead!' from upstairs. They all looked at each other, and then ran up to Bray's bedroom at once. Bray was lying still on the floor, and his daughter lay next to him, her arms round his dead body.

'She's fainted!' said Nicholas to himself, and he quickly

thump a low banging noise

picked her up and started to carry her downstairs.

'Stop that at once!' said his uncle angrily. 'What are you doing?'

'I'm taking Madeline to my house. And don't you try to stop me.'

'You can't do that. This man,' Ralph Nickleby said, **pointing** at Gride, 'is going to be her husband.'

'That's right! Listen to him,' said Gride.

'No, listen to me,' said Nicholas to his uncle. 'The debts that Bray had are cancelled by his death, so there's no need now for Madeline to marry Gride. And, between you and me, I think that *you* should start worrying about *your* debts. Just yesterday I overheard some people talking at the office where I work about one of your investments. I believe you'll soon find out that you've just lost ten thousand pounds, sir.'

'That's not true!' screamed Ralph Nickleby, putting his hand to his heart.

'Oh yes, it is! Your day is past, and night is coming on. Now, will you let me and my sister leave with Madeline?'

point to show where something is with your finger

Leaving the house, Nicholas quickly found a coach, and soon he, Kate, and Madeline were on their way to the house in Bow.

During the next few days, Madeline was very ill and stayed in bed. Kate looked after her and brought her food to bring back her strength. The two young women became the nearest and dearest of friends during that time. But while Madeline was getting better, another person in the house was getting ill – Smike. He was very thin, and he had a cough that was becoming worse and worse. He was also very **weak**, and now couldn't walk from room to room. The doctor came to see him.

'He's had **consumption** for a long time,' he said. 'It's because of all those years of being cold, hungry, and dirty in Yorkshire. He has it very badly now, and it's possible that he'll die of it. I'm afraid there's only one thing that can help him. He must leave the city and go into the country. The air there will be good for him, but it's perhaps already too late.'

So Nicholas, after talking with the Cheerybles, took Smike down to Devon. They rented some rooms in a house very near his father's old home. Nicholas showed Smike all the places that he loved as a child. One afternoon they visited his father's **grave**, under a big tree near the old Nickleby house. But Smike grew weaker and weaker every day. Soon he couldn't leave his bed. So Nicholas sat next to him and talked to him, or read to him, for hours and hours. When Smike's suffering was at its worst, Nicholas was always there to make him more comfortable. Then, one warm, autumn evening, Smike became very much worse. It was clear to both of them that he was dying.

'I'm not afraid to die,' Smike said. 'Because I know that we'll meet again.'

weak not strong

consumption when you are very ill in the chest

grave a hole in the ground where you put a dead body

'Yes, I'm sure that we will,' Nicholas said.

'I'd like to lie in a grave near your father's grave, in that beautiful place under the tree near your old house.'

'I'll make sure that you do.'

'Now I can die happily,' Smike said.

And soon after that, Smike took his last **breath**.

breath when you move air into or out of your body

investment money that you put into a business to make more money

At about the same time, a letter arrived for Ralph Nickleby. While he read it, his face turned white: £10,000 lost in a bad **investment**! It was too cruel. And soon all of London would know this terrible news. His nephew Nicholas knew it already! Ralph Nickleby's hand shook when he put the letter down on the table. Once a rich moneylender, he was now suddenly poor! How could he possibly survive? There was no hope for him.

READING CHECK

Match the first and second parts of these sentences.

a Gride will cancel Bray's debt
b Nicholas tells Madeline that
c Madeline doesn't love
d Nicholas and Kate go to Bray's house
e Nicholas carries Madeline
f Kate looks after Madeline
g Nicholas takes Smike to Devon
h Ralph Nickleby loses £10,000

1 Gride, but wants to help her father.
2 when she is ill in bed.
3 for the good country air.
4 if he marries Bray's daughter.
5 to stop the marriage.
6 in a business that did badly.
7 to a coach.
8 he will help her in any way posssible.

WORD WORK

Find words in the wedding ring to complete the sentences.

a When my sister marries, she wants a white ...wedding... in the village church.
b Stop .... your finger at that poor man with only one eye. It isn't nice.
c What are all those .... from upstairs? Are the boys jumping off the bed onto the floor?
d Lots of poor people became ill with .... in Europe in the 1840s.
e Many little children in Africa are hungry and ...., and can't walk very far.
f Oscar Wilde died in France and his .... is in Paris.
g Take a deep .... and then put your head under the water for a minute.
h Nicholas's father made a bad .... and so he died a poor man.

GUESS WHAT

What happens in the next chapter? Are these sentences true or false? Tick the boxes.

	True	False
a Ralph Nickleby meets a person from his past.	☐	☐
b Ralph Nickleby tells everyone that he's sorry for everything.	☐	☐
c Madeline becomes very ill again.	☐	☐
d Ralph Nickleby comes to a bad end.	☐	☐
e The Cheerybles make a bad investment and their business soon closes.	☐	☐
f Squeers goes to prison and Dotheboys Hall closes.	☐	☐
g Nicholas buys his father's old house in Devon.	☐	☐

Chapter eight

The church bells ring

Early on the day after Ralph Nickleby learnt of his bad investment, Charles Cheeryble went to see him.

'I have some very important news for you,' Charles said as soon as he arrived.

'If it's about my bad investment, I already know it,' answered Ralph Nickleby quickly.

'No, it's something different.'

'I'm not interested.'

'Look, I wanted to tell you this news in a kind way, so that you can put right what you've done wrong while there's still time. Next time it'll be harder,' said Charles when he left.

Later that day Ralph Nickleby went out for a walk. While he was walking, he thought darkly about the last few days. Nothing was going right. And at every wrong turn along the way, there was Nicholas! After an hour, he saw that he was near Snawley's house. Snawley often did little jobs for him, like when he agreed to be Smike's father for the day. But when Ralph Nickleby knocked on Snawley's front door, there was no answer. He knocked again, and saw someone looking down from an upstairs window and then quickly moving away. In the end, Mrs Snawley came to the door.

'He's not here,' she said. 'He's gone out.'

'But I can see him standing at the window upstairs,' replied Nickleby laughing uneasily.

'It's not him. Please leave us alone,' she said, closing the door in his face.

Ralph Nickleby still wanted to talk to someone. He decided to walk to Gride's house. He arrived there after another hour's walk, and knocked a number of times on the door. But there was no answer; Gride also was not at home to answer him.

That evening there was a loud knock at Ralph Nickleby's front door. It was Ned Cheeryble.

'Please come with me immediately,' he said. 'Now we have more news to tell you, and it's not good, I'm afraid.'

'I can see that you people won't leave me alone until you've told me everything,' Ralph Nickleby replied, putting on his coat and hat and following Ned Cheeryble to his house.

At the Cheerybles' place Ralph Nickleby sat down by the fire. He saw that another man was sitting quietly in a big chair far from the fire, but the room was too dark to see his face clearly.

'Mr Nickleby, I'm sorry to tell you that a young man has just died, a young man who needed your love and help more than any other,' began Charles.

'Ha! Do you mean that Nicholas is dead?' said Nickleby. 'But this is good news, not bad news.'

At this, the person in the chair stood up, and now Ralph Nickleby could see his face in the light from the fire.

'You know this gentleman, I believe,' said Charles Cheeryble. 'It's Mr Brooker, who worked for you a long time ago.'

'Yes, of course I know him. What are you doing here?' he said turning to Brooker.

'Mr Nickleby, the young man that Mr Cheeryble talked of who is now dead . . .'

'Yes? What about him?'

'. . . he was your only son.'

'That's not true!' cried Ralph Nickleby.

'But it is,' said Brooker, and he went on.

'As a young man you were secretly married and had a son. Your marriage was unhappy because you married your wife for her money, and her parents didn't let her have it when they learnt of her secret wedding. After you separated, your wife took her baby son with her, and went to live with her family. But she became ill and died when the child was four years old. You sent me to get your son, and I brought him to your house. You were away from London for six weeks on business. So I stayed alone with the little boy in the house. Like his mother, the child wasn't very strong, and I called a doctor. The doctor said that the boy needed good country air to survive. So I sent the boy to Dotheboys Hall in Yorkshire, and I paid Squeers myself. I told him that the boy's name was Smike. When you came back home, I told you that the boy became ill and was dead.'

Brooker then turned to the Cheeryble brothers and said, 'I admit now that what I did was bad. I planned to tell Mr Nickleby the true story some time later, and to get money from him before I told him where the boy was. You see he was very cruel to me in the past, and I wanted to have my **revenge** on him.'

'That doesn't matter now. Just tell him what happened later,' said Ned Cheeryble.

'Yes, of course,' said Brooker. 'I paid for Smike to stay at Dotheboys Hall for the next five years. Then I was sent to prison for the next eight years and – for the last three of those years – I couldn't pay for the school. Squeers kept the boy there, but not out of kindness. Smike became the servant of the Squeers family, working for nothing. When I got out of prison last year, I went to Yorkshire to see Smike. I found out that he was now with your nephew, Nicholas.

revenge when you do something bad to someone because they did something bad to you

I followed them to their house in Bow. There I met Nicholas who told me about the sad end of poor Smike, who died of consumption in Devon only yesterday.'

Ralph Nickleby was looking down at his hands all this time. He said nothing. The room was now dark. No one spoke, and then suddenly Nickleby got up and walked quickly out of the room and out of the house. Outside it was a windy night. He went back home. Inside the large, dark, cold house he tried to **imagine** the son that he once had, as a little boy, playing on the floor. He tried to imagine the wife that he once had, making dinner for the three of them. But his eyes came back to his house, empty of love, as it really was. Just then, the church **bells** outside rang midnight.

Nickleby went to the window, and looking up at the bells, he shouted, 'Ring, bells! Ring for the coming in of every year that brings this terrible world nearer to its end!'

imagine to see pictures in your head

bell a metal thing that makes a noise when you move it

The next morning they found him with a **rope** round his neck, **hanging** dead in his kitchen.

Some weeks after Ralph Nickleby's death, Nicholas and Madeline got married, and were very happy. Kate married Frank Cheeryble, the Cheeryble brothers' nephew. He was a friendly young man with the same kind, smiling eyes as his uncles, and he and Nicholas became good friends. After some years, when Charles and Ned Cheeryble stopped working, a new sign went up over the door of their London offices. It said, 'Cheeryble and Nickleby'.

Arthur Gride did not try to marry any more young women. But he came to a bad end: thieves broke into his house one night, stole all his money, and murdered him in his bed while he was sleeping.

Squeers went to prison in the end for his criminal ways, and that was the end of Dotheboys Hall. Before the boys left the school for the last time, they broke as much of the place and the furniture in it as they could. John Browdie helped the smaller boys move to some of the homes in his village, and in other villages that were near. And the Nicklebys and the Browdies often visited each other.

When Nicholas had enough money, he bought his father's old house in Devon, and Kate and Frank bought a house for themselves not far from it. Mrs Nickleby lived some of the time with Kate and the rest of the time with Nicholas. And after some years, there were two groups of children playing in the same places where once Nicholas and Kate played as children.

Newman Noggs went to live in a small house next to Nicholas's house in Devon. When Nicholas and his family were in London, he looked after their country home. When they were in Devon, Newman's greatest joy was to play with the little children.

rope a very thick, strong string

hang to kill someone by putting something around their neck and holding them above the ground

In spring and summer, those children put flowers on a small grave near the house. It lay under a tree, just next to the grave of Nicholas's and Kate's father. And it belonged to the boy that they knew as their **cousin** Smike.

cousin the son (or daughter) of your father's (or mother's) brother (or sister)

READING CHECK

Are these sentences true or false? Tick the boxes.	True	False
a Brooker looked after Ralph Nickleby's son when he was a baby.	☐	☑
b Ralph Nickleby paid for Smike to go to Dotheboys Hall school.	☐	☐
c Brooker tells Ralph Nickleby that his nephew has died.	☐	☐
d Kate marries Charles Cheeryble.	☐	☐
e Nickleby marries Madeline Bray.	☐	☐
f The Nicklebys and the Browdies continue to be friends.	☐	☐
g Smike's grave is in London.	☐	☐
h Newman Noggs goes to live in a house near Nicholas and Kate.	☐	☐

WORD WORK

Nicholas's oldest son, William, is talking to Newman Noggs by Smike's grave. Complete their conversation with the words in the gravestone.

William: Mr Noggs, why didn't Brooker tell Ralph Nickleby the true story about **a)** ..cousin.. Smike sooner?

Newman: He wanted **b)** .... for what Ralph Nickleby did to him earlier.

William: And how did Ralph Nickleby die?

Newman: Well, he took a **c)** .... and he **d)** .... himself with it.

William: And is Smike happy now?

Newman: Yes, William, I **e)** .... that he is. (*He puts his hand to his ear and listens.*) But that's the church **f)** .... ringing seven o'clock. Let's go in.

WHAT NEXT?

Which of these DVDs would you prefer to watch? Why?

Nicholas Nickleby (2003) 132 minutes
with Charlie Hunnam as Nicholas, Jamie Bell as Smike, Jim Broadbent as Squeers, Anne Hathaway as Madeline, Christopher Plummer as Ralph Nickleby. This is a short film version of the main characters and events in the story by Charles Dickens.

The Life and Adventures of Nicholas Nickleby (1983) 9 hours (4 DVDs)
with Nigel Rees as Nicholas and 38 different actors from the Royal Shakespeare Company as all the other 150 characters. Filmed at the Old Vic Theatre in London. This full version of the Dickens story is a theatre adaptation by David Edgar.

What are the good things about reading a story in a book? What are the good things about seeing the film of the book?

Which Dickens story would you like to see as a film, or read as a book, next?

Bleak House – the story of a rich lady who is caught in a loveless marriage, two young cousins who hope to become rich, and a poor young woman who doesn't know who her mother and father were. With Charles Dance and Gillian Anderson.

The Old Curiosity Shop – the story of a girl who travels to the sea with her grandfather after the old man has to give his shop – full of strange old things – to Quilp the moneylender. With Peter Ustinov and Tom Courtenay.

Hard Times – the story of a man who thinks that it's better to follow your head not your heart, but who changes when his son becomes dishonest and his daughter leaves her husband. With Alan Bates and Richard E Grant.

Project A A Minisaga Summary

In the original Charles Dickens book 'Nicholas Nickleby' there are more stories about other characters that are not in this reader.

1 Put these sentences in order to make a very short story – a 'minisaga' – about Madame and Mr Mantalini, two characters from the Dickens book.

- **a** But he spends Madame Mantalini's money freely, so they have debts. ☐
- **b** In the end, the Mantalinis separate – and Mr Mantalini has to work. ☐
- **c** Lazy Mr Mantalini doesn't work. ☐
- **d** Busy Madame Mantalini makes hats for rich Londoners. ☐
- **e** He sends poor Kate to work with them. ☐
- **f** They borrow money from Ralph Nickleby. ☐

2 Put the words in the right order to make a title for the minisaga in Activity 1.

Mantalini/making/How/the/spends/wife/his/that/busy/Alfred/lazy/money/hats/gets/.

....

3 Complete the rules for writing minisagas.

- **a** A minisaga story must be exactly .... words long (it can't be any longer, or any shorter).
- **b** The title of a minisaga cannot be longer than .... words (but it can be shorter if you want).

Read a 100 word summary of the 'Nicholas and Sir Mulberry Hawke' story. Which page in this reader starts the story?

In a large restaurant near the centre of London, Nicholas angrily overhears Mulberry Hawke laughing loudly with different friends about his sister Kate. Nicholas goes to him and tells him to say sorry for his words, but Mulberry Hawke just leaves and goes to his coach, which is waiting for him outside. Nicholas, who is now even angrier, tries to pull him out of his coach. The horse is very frightened, the coach crashes backwards, and Hawke – who is still inside it when it crashes – breaks many bones. Later he says to everybody that Nicholas hurt him in a fight.

The last brawl between Sir Mulberry and his pupil

Take away words from the story in Activity 4 to make it exactly 50 words long.

Write a title for your minisaga in Activity 5. Use these words: *innocent, kiss, laugh, revenge, sister.*

Write a minisaga:

a Summarizing one chapter of this reader.

or

b Summarizing the whole story of this reader.

(Don't forget to give your minisaga a title!)

Project B Writing a Playscript

1 Read the playscript and answer the questions.

Scene 14: Fanny's tea party

FANNY, NICHOLAS, TILDA and JOHN BROWDIE at the kitchen table. On it a plate of bread and butter, teapot, teacups, saucers, milk jug and sugar bowl.

FANNY: (*very sweetly and lovingly*) Mr Nickleby, please have some bread and butter.

NICHOLAS: Thank you. I will.

NICHOLAS eats lots of bread and butter hungrily. JOHN BROWDIE laughs.

JOHN BROWDIE: You won't get fat if you stay in this school!

FANNY: (*angrily*) John, don't speak to Mr Nickleby like that!

TILDA: (*smiling knowingly*) Oh Fanny, shall we leave you and Mr Nickleby together?

NICHOLAS: (*looking surprised and worried*) Oh no. Please don't go. Tilda, tell me what do you do to pass the time in Yorkshire?

TILDA: I like playing cards.

NICHOLAS: (*smiling at her*) Oh, and I'm sure that you're very good at that.

TILDA: (*enjoying herself*) But not as good as you are at it, I'm sure.

FANNY: (*standing up angrily*) Tilda Price, I don't think that's a nice way for you to talk to my special friend, Mr Nickleby. I'm not going to speak to you ever again.

JOHN BROWDIE: (*standing up angrily*) It's time to go, Tilda.

TILDA: (*standing up, laughing*) You'll soon want to be friends again, Fanny.

TILDA and JOHN BROWDIE leave through the door on the right. NICHOLAS stands.

NICHOLAS: (*to the audience*) I must stop trying to being friendly to everyone. It just gets me into trouble.

NICHOLAS leaves through the door on the left. FANNY starts crying.

a Which chapter and page in the story in this book is the scene from?

b Where exactly does it happen?

c Who are the people in this scene? How are their names shown?

d How does the playscript show when people speak, and when they do things?

e Underline the parts of the dialogue (what people say) which are the same in the story.

f What 'props' (things that actors touch and hold) are needed in this scene?

Find the part of the story when Nicholas first sees Madeline. Complete the table.

Book page	Chapter 5, page__________
Place	at ______________________________; the outer office, and CHARLES's inner office
People in this scene	_______________ NICKLEBY, ______________ CHEERYBLE, ____________ CHEERYBLE, and ________________ BRAY
Dialogue already in the story	NICHOLAS: (*to himself*) ____________________________________ ________________ NED: ____________________________________ ________________ NICHOLAS: (*to himself*) ____________________
Some new dialogue	NED: You need to show it to Charles. MADELINE: (*crying*) You must help me! I don't know what to do. NICHOLAS: (*to himself*) She's beautiful! CHARLES: Don't cry, my dear. You'll make yourself ill. CHARLES: Go and get Ned!
Stage directions *(Things that people do)*	*NICHOLAS knocks at CHARLES's office door. He hears ____________.* *NICHOLAS opens the door and goes in. He is ____________ to see that CHARLES is in his office, talking to MADELINE.* *MADELINE is ___________________ a lot.* *Suddenly MADELINE _____________, and falls to the floor.* *NICHOLAS can only stand looking at MADELINE without ___________ ___________________________.* *NED ______________________ into CHARLES's office.* *______________ leaves the room.*
Props	two chairs, a desk, a letter

3 Complete the scene with stage directions and dialogue from the grid in Activity 2.

Scene 48: NICHOLAS SEES MADELINE FOR THE FIRST TIME

At the ______________________. In the outer office, NICHOLAS is standing holding a ____________. NED is passing. Inside CHARLES's office, CHARLES is talking to MADELINE who is sitting in front of him. She is ____________ a lot. We cannot hear them.

NICHOLAS: Ned, What shall I do with this letter?

NED: (*looking at it*) ______________________________. He's in his office, I think.

NED goes off to his office. NICHOLAS knocks at CHARLES's door. There's ____________.

NICHOLAS: (*to the audience*) That's strange. There's no reply. Perhaps he's out. ____.

NICHOLAS opens the door, and goes in. Suddenly we hear CHARLES and MADELINE.

NICHOLAS is surprised ______________________________ talking to MADELINE.

MADELINE: (*crying*) ____.

CHARLES: (*putting his hand on her shoulder*) ______________________________ ______________________.

Suddenly ______________________ and falls to the floor. NICHOLAS ____________ ____.

CHARLES: (*trying to help MADELINE up*) Nicholas, don't just stand there. ____________ ______________. Please!

NICHOLAS: (*to the audience*) ______________________________!

NED ______________________.

NED: (*to NICHOLAS*) ____ ____

NICHOLAS: Yes, of course. (*to the audience*) What a beautiful young lady! __________ ______________________?

NICHOLAS leaves the room looking at MADELINE.

4 Choose a different scene from Nicholas Nickleby and write a playscript of it. Make notes in a table to help you. When you finish, act the scene.

GRAMMAR CHECK

Going to Future: affirmative and negative

We make *going to* future affirmative with the verb am/is/are + going + to + infinitive.

The Cheerybles are going to help Nicholas.

We make *going to* future negative with am not/isn't/aren't + going + to + infinitive.

Madeline isn't going to marry Gride.

We can use *going to* future to talk about intentions.

'I'm going to walk to London,' said Nicholas.

We can also use *going to* future to make predictions.

Smike is very ill, and he's going to die.

Write the words in the correct order to make sentences.

a going / I / show / advertisement / am / to / an / you

I am going to show you an advertisement.

b to / miss / Nicholas / They / going / a lot / are

....

c going / is / Nicholas / to / cost / anything / not / mother / his

....

d is / to / Nicholas / Smike / going / live / with

....

Complete the sentences. Use the affirmative or negative form of *going to* and the verbs in brackets.

a Mrs Nickleby is going to ask (ask) her husband's brother for help.

b He .... (not cry) about his brother's death.

c Mrs Nickleby .... (be) sad when her son leaves.

d Kate Nickleby .... (stay) with her mother and look for work.

e Nicholas .... (try) to get a job with Mr Squeers.

f Kate and her mother .... (not go) to Yorkshire.

g Mr and Mrs Squeers .... (make) the boys suffer.

GRAMMAR CHECK

Gerund as subject or object

We can use the gerund as the subject or object of a verb. To make the gerund, we usually add –ing to the verb, but when a verb ends in a consonant + –e, we remove the e and add –ing.

suffer – Suffering was the only thing in Smike's life. (= subject)

lose – Nobody likes losing. (= object)

The gerund can have its own object.

Squeers was looking forward to beating him later.

3 Complete the sentences with the gerund (*–ing*) form of the verbs in the box.

cry	do	have	help	work	look after	make
paint	smile	talk	~~beat~~	want	work	

a Mr Squeers loved beating the boys at his school.

b Smike liked .... in the Nicklebys' garden.

c The Cheeryble brothers liked .... people.

d .... pictures made some money for Madeline Bray.

e Mr Snawley liked .... little jobs for Ralph Nickleby.

f Fanny Squeers started .... after the tea party.

g Nicholas enjoyed .... a laugh with the Cheeryble brothers.

h Kate went on .... their house comfortable every day.

i Mrs Nickleby preferred .... about the work in the house.

j Everybody began .... when Smike came back to the Nicklebys' house.

k Kate began .... Madeline when she was ill.

l Ralph Nickleby stopped .... to live when he lost his son and his money.

m When the Cheeryble brothers stopped .... , Nicholas worked with their nephew Frank.

GRAMMAR CHECK

Time clauses with before, after, when, and while

Before links a later action with an earlier action.

Before Nicholas got onto the coach, someone pushed a letter into his hand.

After links an earlier action with a later action.

After they first met in the kitchen, Smike followed Nicholas everywhere.

When links two actions close in time, often where the first action is the reason for the second action.

When Nicholas arrived at the inn, Squeers was busy with some new students.

While is used for two actions happening at the same time, or for a background action that is going on when something else happens.

While Madeline was getting better, Smike was getting ill.

We can put *before, after, when,* and *while* clauses at the end of the sentence. In this case, we do not use a comma.

Smike was getting ill while Madeline was getting better.

Complete the text with *before, after, when, or while.*

a) ...When... he was a young man, Ralph Nickleby married secretly and had a son. b) .... Ralph and his wife separated, she took their son home to her family. She died c)............ the boy was four years old. Mr Brooker went to get the boy. He took the boy to Dotheboys Hall d) .... Ralph was away from London. e) .... Ralph came home, Mr Brooker told him that the boy was dead.

Smike worked as a servant at Dotheboys Hall f) .... Mr Brooker was in prison. g) .... he met Nicholas at the school, they became friends. Then Nicholas left. Two days later, h) .... Nicholas was sleeping in a barn, Smike found him.

After two weeks in London, Squeers found Smike. i) .... Smike could escape, Squeers pushed him into a coach. j) .... John Browdie heard about this, he helped Smike to escape. But Smike became ill.

k) .... Ralph Nickleby learnt that his son was dead, he hanged himself.

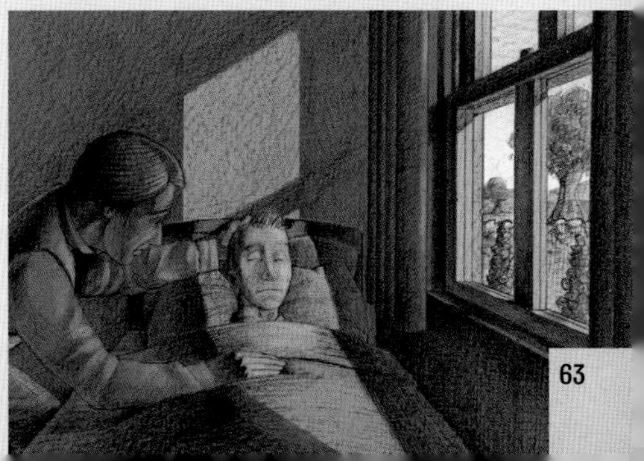

GRAMMAR CHECK

Comparative adjectives

We use a comparative adjective + than to say that two people or things are different in some way.

Nicholas Nickleby was kinder than his brother Ralph.

To make comparative adjectives, we add –er to most short adjectives.	*old – older*
When adjectives finish in –e, we add –r.	*late – later*
When adjectives finish in a consonant + y, we change the y to i and add –er.	*happy – happier*
When adjectives finish in a short vowel + consonant, we double the consonant and add –er.	*big – bigger*
With adjectives of three syllables or more, we put more before the adjective.	*exhausted – more exhausted*

5 Complete the sentences. Use the comparative form of the adjectives in brackets.

- **a** Arthur Gride was much ..older.. (old) than Madeline Bray.
- **b** Nicholas was .... (kind) to Smike than Squeers was.
- **c** Madeline was .... (beautiful) than Fanny.
- **d** Ned was .... (fat) than his brother Charles.
- **e** The Brays were .... (poor) than the Cheerybles.
- **f** Nicholas was .... (strong) than Squeers.
- **g** When Nicholas came back to London, Kate was .... (happy) to see him than Ralph Nickleby was.
- **h** The house in Bow was .... (comfortable) than Dotheboys Hall.
- **i** The Squeers's food was .... (nice) than the boys' food.
- **j** Madeline's life was .... (difficult) than Nicholas's life.
- **k** Fanny and Browdie were .... (angry) than Tilda.

GRAMMAR CHECK

Imperatives

We use imperatives to give instructions, orders, or invitations, or to make offers.

They heard a shout: 'Stop!'

Please come to London as my friend.

Allow us to help you!

Don't worry about anything.

Affirmative imperatives look the same as the infinitive without *to*.

Well, Smike, explain yourself!

Negative imperatives start with do not or don't + infinitive without *to*.

Don't call a doctor; they're very expensive in London.

Choose the correct word or words to complete the Dotheboys School rules.

a ***Get up/Don't get up*** *early in the morning.*
b ***Eat/Don't eat*** *too much.*
c ***Do/Don't do*** *what you are told.*
d ***Run/Don't run*** *away.*

Complete the sentences with the imperatives in the box.

leave	come	don't be	go	don't think
don't worry	let	~~take~~	don't marry	

a '.Take. some money, and my stick,' said John Browdie.
b '............... afraid of me,' Nicholas said to Smike.
c '............... badly of my father,' said Madeline.
d 'Please .... us alone,' Mrs Snawley told Ralph Nickleby.
e '............... about this young lady,' said Ned to Nicholas.
f '............... Gride just because your father tells you to,' Nicholas begged Madeline.

g 'Please .... me come to London with you,' Smike said to Nicholas.
h 'My dearest son, ... to your father,' said Mr Snawley to Smike.
i '............... from this house at once,' said Nicholas.

GRAMMAR CHECK

Verb + preposition: for, to, about, and at

Some verbs are often followed by specific prepositions.

Mrs Squeers was waiting for them.

Nicholas Nickleby listened to his uncle.

Tilda and Fanny talked about the shops in London.

Nicholas smiled at Madeline.

Other examples are:

pay for, look for

agree to, speak to

hear about, worry about

shout at, look at

8 Choose the correct word to complete the sentences.

- **a** The Cheeryble brothers decided ....on.... (on/for) a clever plan.
- **b** In Devon, Nicholas worried .... (at/about) Smike.
- **c** 'Someone will pay .... (about/for) this!' said Squeers angrily.
- **d** The little man listened .... (at/to) Nicholas carefully.
- **e** They were all laughing .... (for/at) a story that Tilda was telling.
- **f** Nicholas sat by Smike's bed and read .... (about/to) him for hours.
- **g** 'Don't think .... (about/for) escaping,' said Squeers cruelly.

9 Complete the sentences with the correct preposition.

- **a** Nicholas thought, 'We'll go and look ....for.... Newman Noggs.'
- **b** Nicholas and Spike travelled .... London.
- **c** 'I heard .... Squeers locking you away,' said John Browdie to Smike.
- **d** While Nicholas was at the Brays' house, Bray shouted .... him.
- **e** Bray agreed .... the marriage of his daughter to Arthur Gride.
- **f** Smike looked .... Nicholas everywhere.
- **g** Madeline smiled .... Nicholas happily.

GRAMMAR CHECK

Prepositions of place

We use prepositions of place to say where things are.

above | behind | between
in | in front of | near
next to | on

Complete the text. Use the prepositions in the box.

above	behind	in	between	in front of
in	~~near~~	next to	on	in front of	on

Nicholas, Madeline, and Kate are a) ..near.. the top of the stairs. Nicholas is b) .... the window, and Madeline is c) .... his arms. Kate stands d) .... Nicholas. She has a hat e) .... her head. f) .... the bedroom, we can see four people. Mr Bray is lying dead g) .... the floor, h) .... the door. He is i) .... Mr Gride and Ralph Nickleby. Ralph Nickleby is j) .... Mr Gride and the servant. He has one hand k) .... his head.

DOMINOES Your Choice

Read *Dominoes* for pleasure, or to develop language skills. It's your choice.

Each *Domino* reader includes:

- a good story to enjoy
- integrated activities to develop reading skills and increase vocabulary
- task-based projects – perfect for CEFR portfolios
- contextualized grammar activities

Each *Domino* pack contains a reader, and an excitingly dramatized audio recording of the story

If you liked this *Domino*, read these:

The Turn of the Screw

Henry James

A young woman arrives at a large country house. Her job is to look after the two children who live there, but she soon discovers that there is something very strange about both the house and the children. The longer she stays, the more she feels that the two children are in danger – or is it that the children are the danger, and the person in danger is herself?

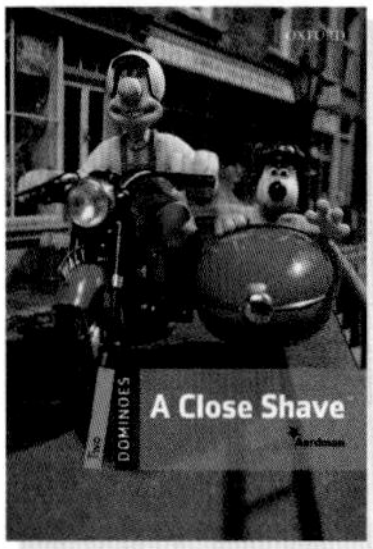

A Close Shave™

Aardman

When Wallace the inventor meets Wendolene in her wool shop, he falls in love with her at once. But why does her dog, Preston, hate Wallace's dog, Gromit?

Then, after Wallace's new sheep-shaving and pullover-making machine falls into the wrong hands, things start to go very wrong. Can Gromit save Wallace from the danger of a 'close shave'?

	CEFR	Cambridge Exams	IELTS	TOEFL iBT	TOEIC
Level 3	B1	PET	4.0	57-86	550
Level 2	A2–B1	KET-PET	3.0-4.0	–	390
Level 1	A1–A2	YLE Flyers/KET	3.0	–	225
Starter & Quick Starter	A1	YLE Movers	1.0–2.0	–	–

You can find details and a full list of books and teachers' resources on our website:
www.oup.com/elt/gradedreaders